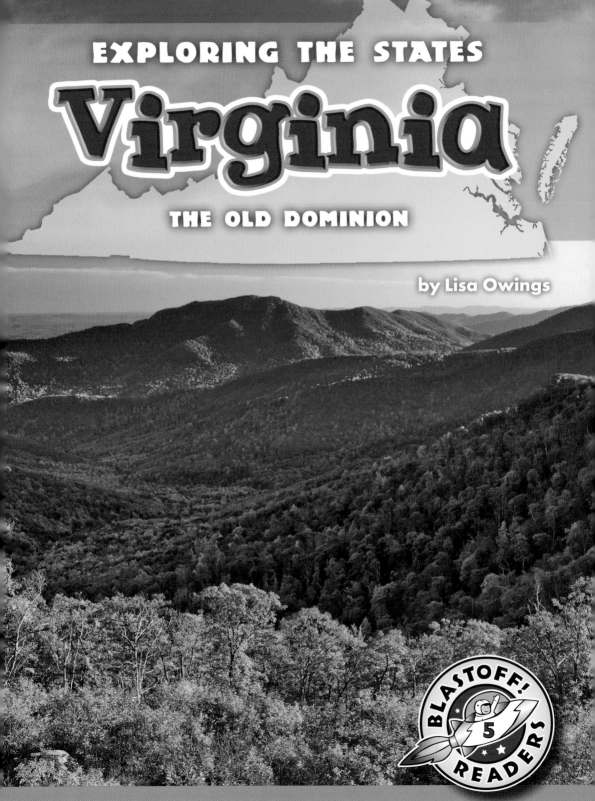

EXPLORING THE STATES

Virginia

THE OLD DOMINION

by Lisa Owings

BELLWETHER MEDIA · MINNEAPOLIS, MN

Note to Librarians, Teachers, and Parents:

Blastoff! Readers are carefully developed by literacy experts and combine standards-based content with developmentally appropriate text.

Level 1 provides the most support through repetition of high-frequency words, light text, predictable sentence patterns, and strong visual support.

Level 2 offers early readers a bit more challenge through varied simple sentences, increased text load, and less repetition of high-frequency words.

Level 3 advances early-fluent readers toward fluency through increased text and concept load, less reliance on visuals, longer sentences, and more literary language.

Level 4 builds reading stamina by providing more text per page, increased use of punctuation, greater variation in sentence patterns, and increasingly challenging vocabulary.

Level 5 encourages children to move from "learning to read" to "reading to learn" by providing even more text, varied writing styles, and less familiar topics.

Whichever book is right for your reader, Blastoff! Readers are the perfect books to build confidence and encourage a love of reading that will last a lifetime!

This edition first published in 2014 by Bellwether Media, Inc.

No part of this publication may be reproduced in whole or in part without written permission of the publisher. For information regarding permission, write to Bellwether Media, Inc., Attention: Permissions Department, 5357 Penn Avenue South, Minneapolis, MN 55419.

Library of Congress Cataloging-in-Publication Data

Owings, Lisa.
Virginia / by Lisa Owings.
    pages cm. – (Blastoff! readers. Exploring the states)
Includes bibliographical references and index.
Summary: "Developed by literacy experts for students in grades three through seven, this book introduces young readers to the geography and culture of Virginia"–Provided by publisher.
ISBN 978-1-62617-046-9 (hardcover : alk. paper)
1. Virginia–Juvenile literature. I. Title.
F226.3.O85 2014
975.5–dc23

2013007778

Printed in the United States of America, North Mankato, MN.

Table of Contents

Where Is Virginia?	4
History	6
The Land	8
The Shenandoah Valley	10
Wildlife	12
Landmarks	14
Richmond	16
Working	18
Playing	20
Food	22
Festivals	24
Pocahontas	26
Fast Facts	28
Glossary	30
To Learn More	31
Index	32

Where Is Virginia?

Did you know?
Virginia shares a small part of its border with the national capital. Washington, D.C. sits on the north shore of the Potomac River between Virginia and Maryland.

West Virginia

Kentucky

Tennessee

Virginia sits in the middle of the United States' East Coast. It shares a border with North Carolina to the south. The state touches Tennessee in the southwest. Kentucky lies on the other side of the western mountains. Virginia's northwestern border follows the curve of West Virginia. Maryland lies across the Potomac River to the northeast.

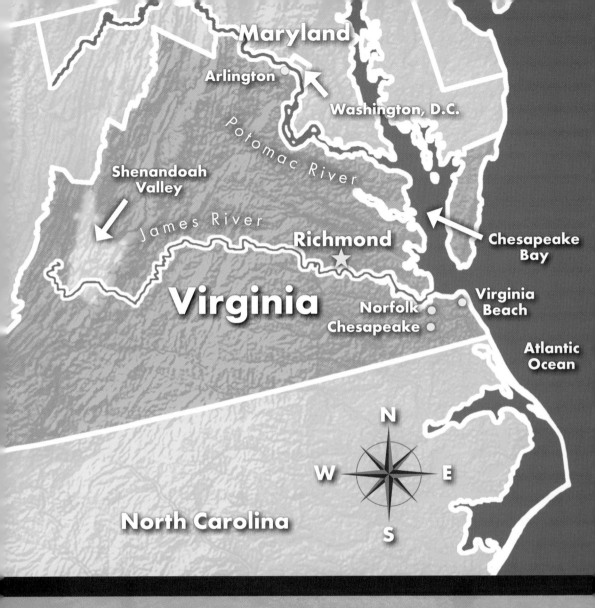

The Chesapeake Bay separates Virginia's mainland from the Eastern Shore. The Eastern Shore is a narrow strip of land on the Delmarva **Peninsula**. The Atlantic Ocean shaped the **inlets** and islands along the eastern coast. Richmond is the state capital. The city was built along the James River in eastern Virginia.

History

Native Americans came to Virginia as early as 12,000 years ago. In 1607, English **colonists** founded Jamestown. They soon began to fight with the Native Americans. The settlers also struggled with hunger and disease. In 1624, Virginians came under British rule. They fought for independence during the **Revolutionary War** in the late 1700s. Virginia became the tenth state in 1788.

Revolutionary
War

Virginia Timeline!

1607: English colonists arrive in Virginia and settle in Jamestown.

1776: Virginian Thomas Jefferson writes the Declaration of Independence.

1788: Virginia becomes the tenth state.

1789: Virginian George Washington becomes the first President of the United States.

1801: Thomas Jefferson becomes the third President of the United States.

1861-1865: Virginia and other southern states fight for independence from the northern states in the Civil War.

1959: African American and white students in Virginia are allowed to attend school together for the first time.

1990: L. Douglas Wilder becomes the first African American governor in the nation.

2001: Terrorists crash an airplane into the Pentagon, the Department of Defense headquarters in Arlington.

George Washington

Civil War

L. Douglas Wilder

The Land

Virginia's landscape is mountainous in the west. The east is laced with rivers and bays. The Appalachian Mountains rise along the state's borders with Kentucky and West Virginia. Dense forests grow on their slopes. East of the mountains lies the Piedmont **Plateau**. Farms dot the rolling green hills of this region.

Coastal **plains** extend from the Piedmont to the Atlantic. The James, York, Rappahannock, and Potomac Rivers widen as they flow over the plains toward the Chesapeake Bay. South of the James River lies the Great Dismal Swamp. Beaches, small islands, and **lagoons** line the Atlantic coast.

Great Dismal Swamp

James River

Virginia's Climate
average °F

spring
Low: 45°
High: 67°

summer
Low: 65°
High: 85°

fall
Low: 49°
High: 69°

winter
Low: 30°
High: 48°

The Shenandoah Valley

The Shenandoah Valley lies in the Appalachian Mountains. The Shenandoah River flows through it to meet the Potomac in the north. The Blue Ridge Mountains form the eastern slope of the valley. Shenandoah National Park stretches across their peaks. The valley's Skyline Drive offers spectacular views. Azalea bushes and dogwood trees bloom throughout the park.

The valley also features interesting rock formations. A natural stone bridge crosses Cedar Creek at the southern end of the valley. The limestone Natural Chimneys were named for their unusual shapes. The Luray Caverns are also nestled in the valley. **Stalactites** and other limestone formations take shape within these caves.

Luray Caverns

fun fact

One of the Luray Caverns houses the largest musical instrument in the world. The Stalacpipe Organ plays by striking stalactites with rubber mallets.

fun fact

The star-nosed mole gets its name from the 22 pink tentacles that surround its nose. The tentacles are extremely sensitive. They help the nearly blind mole explore its world.

Virginia provides habitats for a wide range of animals. Bobcats chase deer and smaller prey through the forests. The Appalachians are home to the **endangered** snowshoe hare. Black bears can be found in the mountains and the Great Dismal Swamp. The star-nosed mole is a more unusual-looking swamp dweller.

bobcat

snowshoe hare

barking tree frog

sea turtle

Eagles and peregrine falcons peer down from the skies. Red cardinals are easy to spot in the forests. Virginia nights come alive with bats, barking tree frogs, and rattlesnakes. The state's rivers and lakes hold bass and perch. Sea turtles sometimes make their way into Chesapeake Bay and coastal waters.

13

Landmarks

Many visitors to Virginia are interested in the state's history. They can tour Historic Jamestowne for a peek into the lives of the first English settlers. The Jamestown Settlement has **replicas** of the ships they arrived in. Presidential homes are other popular landmarks. George Washington's Mount Vernon home was built along the Potomac. Thomas Jefferson's Monticello **plantation** is near Charlottesville.

Arlington National Cemetery honors those who served in the U.S. military. Nearby, the American flag flies above the U.S. Marine Corps War Memorial. Shenandoah National Park attracts visitors to the Blue Ridge Mountains. Off the coast, Chincoteague Island is known for its relaxing waterside inns.

Jamestown Settlement

U.S. Marine Corps War Memorial

Did you know?

Williamsburg is home to the world's largest living history museum. Costumed actors and more than 500 historic buildings bring Colonial Williamsburg to life.

Colonial Williamsburg

Richmond

Richmond was founded in 1737 along the James River. The city became the state capital in 1780. During most of the **Civil War**, it also served as the capital of the **Confederacy**. The people of Richmond set fire to their city as Northern forces took over in 1865. This prevented the North from using their stored supplies.

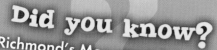

Did you know?
Richmond's Monument Avenue is lined with statues of Civil War heroes such as Robert E. Lee and Stonewall Jackson.

fun fact

Famous writer Edgar Allan Poe grew up in Richmond. In 1922, the city opened a museum to share his life and work.

The city recovered quickly after the war. Today, more than one million people live in and around Richmond. Many of them work in the tall buildings downtown. In their free time, they enjoy the city's museums and historic sites.

Working

Most Virginians have **service jobs**. Some work in stores and hospitals. Those who work in hotels, restaurants, and museums serve the many **tourists** who visit the state. Factory workers make food products, medicines, and electronics. Many people who live near Washington, D.C. work for the U.S. government.

Many farmers in the state raise chickens, turkeys, and cattle. Those in the south and east enjoy long growing seasons. They tend crops of tobacco, tomatoes, and peanuts. Many farmers in the state raise chickens, turkeys, and cattle. Fishers harvest oysters and blue crabs from the Chesapeake Bay. Tuna and swordfish are caught in Atlantic waters.

Where People Work in Virginia

manufacturing
6%

farming and
natural resources
1%

services
75%

government
18%

Playing

Adventurous Virginians love to spend time outdoors. Canoeists and kayakers paddle down the state's many rivers. Thrill-seekers raft the James River rapids. The Appalachian Trail offers **scenic** and challenging hikes through the mountains. Skiers fly down the snow-covered slopes in winter. Come summer, golfers haul their clubs to courses throughout the state.

Popular vacation spots include Assateague and Chincoteague Islands. Families enjoy day trips to Colonial Williamsburg. For an evening out, Virginians take in operas, ballets, and concerts. Sports fans attend college football and basketball games.

kayaking

The Appalachian National Scenic Trail winds for 2,184 miles (3,515 kilometers) through the mountains along the East Coast. One-fourth of the trail lies in Virginia.

Spoonbread

Ingredients:

1 15-ounce can corn, drained

1 15-ounce can creamed corn

1 cup sour cream

2 eggs, beaten

1/2 cup (1 stick) butter, melted

1 8.5-ounce box corn muffin or cornbread mix

1/2 teaspoon salt

1/4 teaspoon pepper

Cinnamon

Directions:

1. Preheat oven to 350°F.

2. Combine all ingredients except cinnamon in a large bowl.

3. Place mixture in an oven-safe baking dish. Bake for 45 minutes.

4. Serve warm with a sprinkling of cinnamon.

Brunswick stew

fun fact

Brunswick stew is a hearty Virginia meal. It was originally made with squirrel meat.

Virginia's farms and waters offer plenty of fresh food. People along the coast enjoy seafood. Chesapeake Bay blue crabs are especially popular just after they shed their shells in the summer. Crab cakes are year-round favorites. Virginia is also known for its oysters. These salty morsels are best slurped raw from their shells.

Country hams are a Virginia specialty. Those made in the town of Smithfield are famous nationwide. Spoonbread is a classic Southern side dish made with cornmeal. In summer, Virginians flock to the Shenandoah Valley to pick sweet peaches from the orchards.

Festivals

Virginia Gold Cup

Year-round festivals bring Virginians together. By March, sap is running through the sugar maples. People can watch as maple syrup is made at the Highland Maple Festival in Monterey. April brings Historic Garden Week. For eight days, Virginians can tour gardens and flower-filled homes throughout the state.

Old Fiddlers'
Convention

fun fact

In July, Virginians watch cowboys round up the wild ponies on Assateague Island. The ponies then swim to Chincoteague Island. There, some of them are sold.

The Virginia Gold Cup horse races take place in May. Thousands turn out in fancy clothes and hats for the event. They watch horses race over fences and other obstacles. Fans of mountain music head to Galax for the Old Fiddlers' Convention in August. In October, seafood lovers feast on oysters at the Chincoteague Oyster Festival.

Pocahontas defending
John Smith

Native Americans were living in Virginia when the colonists arrived in 1607. Chief Powhatan led the tribes in the area. Pocahontas was Powhatan's daughter. She befriended John Smith, one of the colony's leaders. Smith later claimed Pocahontas saved his life. He said she placed her head over his just before Powhatan's men would have killed him.

In 1613, some of the colonists kidnapped Pocahontas. They used her to demand weapons and tools from Powhatan. While Pocahontas was held prisoner, colonist John Rolfe fell in love with her. Pocahontas married him and made peace between her people and the English. The story of Pocahontas is part of the rich history that makes Virginians proud.

fun fact

The Disney version of this story shows Pocahontas as a young woman. However, she was around 10 years old when she first met John Smith.

Fast Facts About Virginia

Virginia's Flag

Virginia's flag shows the state seal against a dark blue background. In the center, a goddess of virtue stands over a fallen tyrant, or cruel ruler. The state motto reads across the bottom of the seal. This flag design was adopted in 1861.

State Flower
American dogwood

State Nicknames:	The Old Dominion Mother of Presidents
State Motto:	*Sic Semper Tyrannis*; "Thus Always to Tyrants"
Year of Statehood:	1788
Capital City:	Richmond
Other Major Cities:	Virginia Beach, Norfolk, Chesapeake, Arlington
Population:	8,001,024 (2010)
Area:	40,599 square miles (105,151 square kilometers); Virginia is the 35th largest state.
Major Industries:	government, tourism, mining, farming, fishing, manufacturing
Natural Resources:	coal, stone, clay
State Government:	100 representatives; 40 senators
Federal Government:	11 representatives; 2 senators
Electoral Votes:	13

State Bird
northern cardinal

State Animal
American foxhound

Glossary

Civil War—a war between the northern (Union) and southern (Confederate) states that lasted from 1861 to 1865

colonists—people who settle new land for their home country

Confederacy—the southern states that fought against the northern states in the American Civil War

endangered—at risk of becoming extinct

inlets—narrow bodies of water that reach inland from the sea

lagoons—shallow bodies of water protected by a barrier of sand or coral

native—originally from a specific place

peninsula—a section of land that extends out from a larger piece of land and is almost completely surrounded by water

plains—large areas of flat land

plantation—a large farm that grows coffee, cotton, rubber, or other crops; plantations are mainly found in warm climates.

plateau—an area of flat, raised land

replicas—exact copies of something

Revolutionary War—the war between 1775 and 1783 in which the United States fought for independence from Great Britain

scenic—providing beautiful views of the natural surroundings

service jobs—jobs that perform tasks for people or businesses

stalactites—icicle-shaped formations that hang from the ceilings of caves

tourists—people who travel to visit another place

To Learn More

AT THE LIBRARY

Cunningham, Kevin. *The Virginia Colony*. New York, N.Y.: Children's Press, 2012.

DeAngelis, Gina. *Virginia*. New York, N.Y.: Children's Press, 2009.

Edison, Erin. *Pocahontas*. North Mankato, Minn.: Capstone Press, 2013.

ON THE WEB

Learning more about Virginia is as easy as 1, 2, 3.

1. Go to www.factsurfer.com.

2. Enter "Virginia" into the search box.

3. Click the "Surf" button and you will see a list of related Web sites.

With factsurfer.com, finding more information is just a click away.

Index

activities, 14, 17, 20, 24
Appalachian Trail, 20, 21
Arlington National Cemetery, 14
capital (see Richmond)
Chesapeake Bay, 5, 8, 13, 19, 23
Chincoteague Island, 14, 20, 25
Chincoteague Oyster Festival, 25
climate, 9
Colonial Williamsburg, 15, 20
festivals, 24-25
food, 22-23, 25
Highland Maple Festival, 24
Historic Garden Week, 24
Historic Jamestowne, 14
history, 6-7, 14, 15, 16, 17, 27
Jamestown Settlement, 6, 7, 14
landmarks, 11, 14-15
landscape, 8-11
location, 4-5
Luray Caverns, 11
Monticello, 14

Mount Vernon, 14
Old Fiddlers' Convention, 25
Pocahontas, 26-27
Potomac River, 4, 5, 8, 11, 14
Richmond, 5, 16-17
Shenandoah Valley, 5, 10-11, 14, 23
sports, 20
U.S. Marine Corps War Memorial, 14
Virginia Gold Cup, 24, 25
wildlife, 12-13
working, 17, 18-19

The images in this book are reproduced through the courtesy of: S. Borisov, front cover (bottom), pp. 10-11; Hulton Archive/ Stringer/ Getty Images, p. 6; (Collection)/ Prints & Photographs Division/ Library of Congress, p. 7 (left); De Agostini Picture Library/ Getty Images, p. 7 (middle); Fredrick Watkins, Jr./ Ebony Collection/ Associated Press, p. 7 (right); Nojustice, p. 8 (small); JacobH, pp. 8-9; George Allen Penton, p. 11 (small); Visuals Unlimited, Inc./ Ken Catania/ Getty Images, p. 12 (small); J & C Sohns/ Tier und Naturfotografie/ SuperStock, pp. 12-13; Tom Reichner, p. 13 (top); Steve Bower, p. 13 (middle); Natursports, p. 13 (bottom); Photoshot Holdings Ltd./ Alamy, p. 14 (bottom); Vacclav, p. 14 (top); David Ball/ Alamy, p. 15; Dmvphotos, pp. 16-17; Alfred Wekelo, p. 16 (top); Traveler1116 RM/ Alamy, p. 16 (bottom); Anneka, p. 18; Photri Images/ SuperStock, p. 19; Oleg Zabielin, p. 20 (small); James Carroll Richardson/ Age Fotostock/ SuperStock, pp. 20-21; Maryellen Baker/ Getty Images, p. 22; John T. Fowler/ Alamy, p. 23 (top); Steve Lovegrove, p. 23 (bottom); Mark Goldman/ Icon SMI 749/ Newscom, pp. 24-25; AP Photo/ Andres R. Alonso/ Associated Press, p. 25 (top); Paul J. Richards/ AFP/ Getty Images/ Newscom, p. 25 (bottom); North Wind Picture Archives/ Alamy, p. 26; Walt Disney Pictures/ Album/ Newscom, p. 27; Trubach, p. 28 (top); Cheryl E. Davis, p. 28 (bottom); Bonnie Taylor Barry, p. 29 (left); Steve Shott/ Getty Images, p. 29 (left).